How to Write a CV (Curriculum Vitae) and Cover Letter

An Essential CV Writing Guide

by Hugh Kirkpatrick

Table of Contents

Introduction

CV stands for *Curriculum Vitae,* which is Latin for [the] course [of my] life. In the United States, the CV format is used during the application process for teaching positions, fellowships, positions in the medical profession, positions in academia, and jobs in the research divisions of private industries. Unlike a resume, the CV format can be (and often is) longer than just one or two pages. It may include information not usually found on resumes such as theses written, works published and research undertaken. CVs don't have to be flashy nor should they be, but they should reflect an accurate and complementary account of the journey you've taken to arrive at a point where you feel you're a good candidate for the job to which you're applying.

If your prospective employer requires you to submit a CV, then it's important to be diligent and follow all the appropriate guidelines throughout the CV writing process. While there are no iron-clad prescriptive rules regarding font size, font type, the order in which you present the material etc. there are certain stylistic and content related norms that should be followed when using this format. This book will walk you through the process of creating a professional CV that will communicate your accomplishments and impress your prospective employer.

Chapter 1: What to Include in Your CV

CVs should be customized to show you qualify for the positions to which you're applying. Customization will take time, but your odds of making a strong impression increase significantly if your prospective employer has a clear idea of how you'd fit into her specific operation in her specific company.

The content of your CV will also vary depending on your level of academic achievement and the nature of the positions you've held in the past. If your prospective employer has not laid out specific expectations for the content and formatting of your CV, then you should begin by adding as much content as is appropriate for the CV format, then tailoring and structuring the sequence of your content in a way that prioritizes the elements most relevant to the job for which you're applying:

Essential Content

Taking the top spot of your CV is your **name** and **relevant contact information** such as your address (snail mail and email) and your phone number. If you are applying for a position outside of the United States then you should get clarification on the relevant customs for that country. Some countries require CVs to list the applicant's gender, date of birth, marital status, and even the names of the applicant's children.

Include a section on your **academic history**. The names of the schools you attended, the dates in which you attended these schools, and the degrees or certifications earned should all go in the academic history section.

CVs, more so than resumes, tend to feature in detail the **distinctions and experiences** related to one's academic history. It may include information on your thesis or dissertation, including the thesis title, the name of your advisor, and a few sentences explaining the nature of the work itself. Your CV may also include detailed information about any research work you contributed to, including any publications that resulted from the research. When citing "Research Experience," be sure to specify when and where the research was conducted, and with whom. If it applies to you, add a separate section to list and explain any honors and awards you received, such as dean's list standings, scholarships, fellowships, association memberships, and departmental recognitions.

Create a separate section in your CV to list and detail your **teaching positions**. Include the name of the course, the school, and the semester or semesters during which you taught. You can also include any relevant experience you have working as a tutor.

Publications you've authored or co-authored should also be presented in your CV. We will discuss in more detail how to cite your publications later in this book, but you will need to include the name of the paper, the date it was published and any conferences or associations where the paper was presented. Also, include pieces that you are currently working on or pieces that are complete and scheduled for publication.

Professional affiliations or memberships to associations may also warrant their own section on your CV. If you've served on a board of directors for a charity or even for a private company, then this information should also be included.

Your CV should list **work experience**, even if it's not directly relevant to the position you're applying for. List the dates of employment, the name of the employer, along with a brief summary of your job detail and accomplishments.

Your **relevant skills** should also be presented in your CV. Are you an expert programmer in Java, a qualified HR administrator or a master welder? Be sure to include this info.

If you have any relevant or just interesting **extracurricular activities**, then you may want to consider featuring an "Extracurricular Activities" or "Community Involvement" section on your CV. This is where you include any volunteer or service work that you've performed.

Finally, most all CVs should include a "References" section containing the names, titles, and contact information for individuals who've agreed to be your character reference.

Not all CVs require that all the sections listed above be included, but your CV will likely include a mix of these different section types. Again, CVs are best tailored for specific opportunities.

Recommended Format and Length

CVs should be simple, standard, and clear. Times New Roman, Arial, and Calibri are good choices for font style. Your font should be between 10 and 12 points in size with your header information being slightly larger. Each section of your CV should be uniform in style—same font size and style, same indentation, and the same positioning of elements. The names of organizations mentioned in your CV should be italicized. You will have specific accomplishments listed under certain sections of your CV. Use a bullet list to present your accomplishments in an organized and readable way. Bullets "•" or dashes "-" are sufficient to denote each item.

Unlike resumes which are ideally one page and two at the most, CVs are two pages at a minimum and often much longer.

Now that you have a broad idea of how a CV should be curated and which styles employed, let's examine some of these elements in greater detail.

Chapter 2: Structuring the Education, Dissertation, and Fellowships Sections

The CV format is unique in that it's more likely than a resume to have educational detail featured near the beginning of the document. Because the CV format is often required for individuals pursuing academic positions at a university or research positions at a university or elsewhere, highlighting your ability to succeed in an academic setting is paramount.

A good title for this section is "Education." "Academic History" may be a bit too broad, as many elements you will include on your CV will have some connection to academia. This section is about providing a simple record of where you went to school, what you studied, and perhaps a little bit about your thesis or dissertation.

Your degrees should be listed in reverse chronological order (with your most recent or current degree in-progress being featured first). You don't need to feature every college or university you attended, only the ones where you were awarded a degree. Begin your listing by citing your degree, followed by your primary field of study, the institution, and your year of graduation:

M.S.W, Counselling, Washington University, 1995

On the next line, you may include more specific areas of concentration, though this is not something that's necessary to do if you don't want to:

Concentration: Substance Abuse, Family of Origin, Cognitive Behavioral Therapy

And then you may also include a line describing the nature of your thesis or dissertation:

Dissertation: A Study of Substance Abuse Tendencies in the Children of Broken Families

If you're going to add thesis or dissertation details on this section of your CV, then you may want to add a paragraph break after each degree listing and change the font some on the dissertation/thesis title to make it stand out (in terms of formatting). Using bold or italicized text to denote the name of the degree and institution may also come across more professional:

14

M.S.W, Counseling, Washington University, 1995

Concentration: Substance Abuse, Family of Origin, Cognitive Behavioral Therapy

Dissertation: A study of Substance Abuse in Children of Broken Families
Chesterton Smith (chair), Matthew Carlson, and Jennifer Lee

List all the members of your advisory panel, not just the chair. You never know who knows who, and the person evaluating your CV may have a relationship with a non-chair member of your advisory panel.

It is a good idea to write two or three lines describing the nature of your thesis or dissertation under the title, even if you are attaching a copy of its abstract to your CV. This is especially helpful if the title alone doesn't abundantly clarify what your thesis/dissertation is about.

Second only to your academic track record, the nature of your theses and/or dissertations, as well as the reputation of your advisors, will be extremely important to your CV, especially if you're pursuing a job in academia.

After your education section, your CV could progress in a couple different ways depending on what your strongpoints are and the nature of the position you're applying for. When determining the layout of your CV, you should have a strategy in mind for each specific job you're applying for. The order of your content should accommodate this strategy. If you have received at least two prestigious honors, fellowships, awards, or grants, then you may want to consider featuring these in your next section. If you have extensive and impressive teaching experience (especially if you're applying for a teaching position), then perhaps your teaching experience should be featured after the education section. If you've been published (at least once) in a reputable journal, especially if you're at an age or point in your career where such progress is more rare, then maybe you're best having that info lead the charge forward on your CV. Figure out what you want each prospective employer to know about you, prioritize, deliberate a bit, and make the best decision you can.

For your awards, fellowships etc. section, list them in reverse chronological order. Be sure to include the name of the award, fellowship etc. who issued the award, and also be sure to provide a description of the reward where appropriate. Don't assume that anyone knows what an award is, why it's given, and how competitive the selection process is. This is not the time to be modest; you must frankly communicate the prestige and magnitude of your accomplishments:

William Gilmer Perry Essay Award, Georgia Tech, 2001

100$ prize awarded to the undergraduate judged to have completed the best essay in a freshman or sophomore level English class, two winners selected from over one hundred submissions.

Chapter 3: Highlighting Your Teaching Experience and Other Employment

Many jobs requiring CVs either directly or indirectly involve teaching work. Teaching work includes developing syllabi, giving lectures, and grading exams and papers. It's important to use your CV to describe your teaching experience to this point and to present an idea of the subjects you're interested in teaching.

Teaching experience should be presented on your CV in reverse chronological order and you should immediately specify the level of responsibility each position entailed. Teaching roles come in many different shapes and sizes. Here's a general break down:

Teaching Assistants: Supervise small groups of students or labs, may grade exams and papers.

Teaching Associates: Give lectures to the entire class, but no more than 49% of the time, influence the content of the syllabus for a class, may oversee small sections of students or labs, and may grade exams and papers.

Lecturers: Give at least 50% of all classroom lectures, influence the content of the syllabus, may oversee small sections of students or labs, and may grade exams and papers.

Instructors: Give nearly all lectures and substantially influences the content of the syllabus, may oversee small sections of students or labs, and may grade exams and papers.

For each teaching position you held, you will first list your role (Teaching Assistant, Teaching Associate etc.), then the name of the class, and then the course description below the title. If you taught (or helped teach) a course that's not widely known about, then be sure to include details in the course description. It may also help to offset the course description by using a less prominent style of text. Here's an example:

Teaching Associate

The Principles of Euclidian Geometry II

Survey course on the basic applications and derivations of Geometry

University of California, Irvine, Department of Mathematics, 2005 – 2007

Some aspiring teachers will have limited experience teaching, even if they have sufficient expertise in various subject matters. If this is the case, you can list your teaching interest in the form of broad subject areas (Geometry, Differential Equations) or specific course titles. Use the header **"Teaching Interests"** or **"Prepared to Teach."**

If you are applying for a teaching position in an area where you do not have any experience, but are confident of your ability to teach the subject, then you can use your CV to list specific courses you'd want to offer if you were awarded the job.

If your teaching credentials and experience are lengthy, then you may want to consider developing a separate compendium of your teaching credentials and interests to be turned in along with your CV. You may also want to do some research on how to prepare a "teaching portfolio," which is a comprehensive, philosophical testament of your teaching methods, beliefs, and experiences.

Other Professional Experience

If you are a recent masters or doctoral level graduate, then you may not have a whole lot of work experience relevant to the position you're applying for. If this is the case, then consider omitting your professional experience section or placing it near the end of your CV, right before your references. If your professional experience, in your judgment, does much to strengthen your candidacy, then you can give it more prime space on your CV. Be sure to use formatting similar to the formatting you've used elsewhere on your CV.

Typically, the CV format doesn't mesh well with bullet points underneath Professional Experience. If you're applying to be a Classics Professor at Rice University, then it's unlikely that your stellar performance as a beautician at the Macy's makeup counter is going to weigh in on your current pursuit. If you decide to list previous jobs, veer towards keeping the listings brief, just the name of the company, position held and dates employed should suffice under most circumstances.

Chapter 4: Showcasing Your Published Work and Research

In academic and research oriented professions, there is enormous pressure to be published, especially in reputable, peer reviewed books and journals. Publications demonstrate your ability to make an impact in your profession. The publication section of your CV should give your prospective employer an idea of the direction in which your research is proceeding and whether your trajectory will mesh well with their organization or department.

Publications should be listed in reverse chronological order and fully cited. If you have an exceptionally noteworthy publication, such as a refereed article or a book chapter in an edited volume, then you may want to try and distinguish this publication from others that appear in your CV.

When you cite books or journal articles in your CV, use the standard bibliographic conventions appropriate for your field. Here are some examples of how various publication types are typically formatted:

Co-Authored Article

Andrew Thomas and William O'Hare, "Challenges in Hygiene During the Medieval Era," Medieval History Journal, 93 (June 2001): 1498-1555.

Chapter in an Edited Book

"On Viking Cuisine," In A Complete Nordic History, edited by Brian Gunther, Langley: Isotope Press, 2010

Book Reviews:

Review of Scandinavian Dances, by Johnny Dakota, Dancing Centennial Journal 2nd Edition (Spring 2001): 345-501

In today's world, some academic publications may take the form of unfamiliar formats, such as software. It's important for you to use a couple of lines on your CV to explain the significance of any kind of "new media" publication. This is especially important if you're applying to a small department that has not yet standardized this type of "new media." There might be individuals who are going to review your CV, who will need some immediate frame of reference.

Work Awaiting Publication

Your CV can also feature work that is not quite there but on the way, especially if your work in progress is related to the job you aspire to get. It's perfectly acceptable to include items on your CV that are either not yet published, or not even complete. If you've got an article that's been accepted for publication but won't actually be coming out in print for another several weeks or months, then simply replace the publication date in your listing with the word *forthcoming*. Remember, this is only for works that have been submitted <u>and accepted</u>. If your work is still under review, then don't label your piece as *"forthcoming."*

Sometimes graduate students, under the pressure to be published, will seek out opportunities to review books. Sometimes journals will publish these book reviews. This can be a viable strategy if pursued carefully. First of all, you don't want to take too much focus and energy away from your thesis, which really is the lifeblood of academic credibility for a graduate student and should be given the highest of priorities.

Secondly, a bad book review (or even a good one that's perceived to be disingenuous) could put you in a very uncomfortable political situation that you simply don't need when you're first getting started in your career. If you're really interested in writing a book review, then the proper course of action is to involve an advisor to help you in the process.

If you are a new PhD, then like most, you probably don't have any publications yet. It is perfectly acceptable for you to take one or two articles that you've written and submitted to a journal, and feature them in your CV as *work submitted*. This at least shows that you're engaging the publication process and will most likely be published in the future. List your *Works Submitted* in the same bibliographic format as described above.

Some academics like to write all the time, but rarely make the time to send off their articles for review and eventual publication. If this is you, then you should consider developing a section of your CV called *Works in Progress,* where you catalog the prospective titles you've got in the works. If nothing else, this section will give your prospective employer an idea of what subjects interest you.

Research Experience

Depending on which is more relevant to the job for which you're applying, your research experience should be listed either before or after your publications. Research experience is particularly important for those pursuing careers in science.

Your research experience section can be used to expound upon any post-doctoral, doctoral, or undergraduate research. List the names of the institutions where the research took place, the names of the supervising professors, the name of the project and the dates during which it was underway. In a bulleted list describe the key components of your research in more detail. Include the nature of the substances used and the techniques employed if relevant. The particular sequencing you use in your research experience section can take on several different forms. Try to structure your research experience section so that it closely resembles the formatting of the other sections of your CV.

Chapter 5: Listing Relevant Presentations, Affiliations, and Training

Going to conferences in your industry and giving presentations is a mark of professional development and should be recognized on your CV. Moreover, any affiliations relevant to your industry and industry-specific trainings should also bode well for you during the job selection process. These items also deserve space on your CV. List the locations, dates, and titles of the presentations you've given or are scheduled to give.

For professional affiliations, enumerate the names of the organizations, the dates of your involvement, and the details of your involvement, including any special offices you held or accomplishments you made within the organizations. Professional affiliations may also be grouped with university-related associations, such as student council, study groups, committees or other organizations associated with the university. If you made any contribution that had an impact in an organization of this nature worthy of recognition, use bullet points to tout your achievements.

You may have attended professional training at a department in your university or within the jurisdiction of a professional organization or company that has ties to your industry. Whatever the case, it should be notated on your CV. Trainings may include skills training (programming, engineering), teaching, or modules on quantitative methods. Here's an example of a fiction writing training course and how it might look on a CV:

Advanced Novel Writing Workshop

Iowa Summer Writing Festival, Iowa City, 2009

If it's not clear from the title what the training was about, then use bullet points to provide needed detail.

If you speak any foreign languages, the training section of your CV may be a good place to bring attention to your linguistic versatility. In many academic institutions, foundation funding has been issued to reward schools that teach courses in various languages. In many cases, highlighting your polyglot tendencies make you a more attractive candidate.

Chapter 6: Tapping Important References

If you're pursuing work in a highly specialized field (as is often the case with jobs that use the CV format to evaluate candidates) then you're probably operating in a very small world. It's important that you have a lot of people in your corner who can go to bat for you if need be.

References will usually be at the end of a CV, or attached to the CV as an addendum with the title "References." Reference listings on your CV should include the following details:

- Full name

- Title

- Institutional Address

- Telephone address/email/fax

For most academic and research positions at least three references are expected to be listed on your CV. These individuals should know you well. They should also know that they've been included on your CV and have a copy of it for themselves.

Failure to give your references proper notice can lead to unexpected calls and questionable results, so be sure to alert all of your references before you list them.

Chapter 7: How to Write an Impressive Cover Letter

Don't underestimate the importance of a great cover letter. The cover letter will be the first thing your prospective employer sees and the quality of your writing is going to make an impression whether you want it to or not. The efficacy of the CV itself doesn't really hinge on good writing style, but the cover letter does. If you're not the best writer, then work with an editor to produce a cover letter of superior quality.

Your cover letter should be no more than one page in length and should add a human touch to the often lengthy compilation that comprises your CV. It should evoke a sense of confidence and excitement about the position being applied for, along with an understanding of what the job entails. The number one thing most employers are looking for in a cover letter is an indication that the candidate can offer the skills and talents they need.

Your cover letter, if possible, should be addressed directly the person who's going to review your application. If you're not sure who this person is, then you can address your letter: Dear Sir or Madam.

Try to keep your cover letter as natural (though professional) sounding as possible. If you feel that you can't write a good letter without a rudimentary outline to follow, then follow this step-by-step breakdown:

First Paragraph

State the job for which you're applying, how you found out about it, and when you're available to start work.

Second Paragraph

Describe why you're interested in the position, and why you'd like to be a part of the company, university, or government in question.

Third Paragraph

Describe how your particular strong suits could prove advantageous for the organization in question and relate these strong suits, along with your skills, to the specific requirements of the job.

Final Paragraph

Mention any interview dates that *wouldn't* work for you and thank the employer for her time and consideration.

Close the letter with "Yours Sincerely" if you addressed it to a specific person. If you used "Dear Sir or Madam, then close with "Yours faithfully."

If you're submitting your CV by email, then use the body of the email for your cover letter. Generally, email cover letters should be a bit shorter, composed of simple one or two line messages with full line breaks between them. Never write in all caps when writing a cover letter by email unless you're using a well-known acronym.

The same basic rules apply with email when it comes to openings and closings: if you don't know the name of the addressee, use "Dear Sir or Madam" etc. If you get a response and the responding party signs their email with "Dave," then it's ok to address your next email with "Hi Dave." If the person responds to you using the closing "regards," "best," or "kindly," then it's ok for you to follow suit.

Conclusion

Most individuals who find themselves in a position where they need to construct a CV are going to be fairly bright right out of the gate. This is a good thing, because you'll need to use that intellectual acumen to customize and perfect your CV and cover letter, finding the best methods of presentation for each unique employment opportunity. A quick web search will reveal that no two CVs are going to be formatted and sequenced exactly alike. Your first priority with each CV you dispatch is to ensure that it provides evidence of a candidate capable of doing the job at hand.

If you are a recent doctoral or masters graduate then you should have your CV evaluated by a member of your department. Depending on the field, different idiosyncratic styles and tendencies become established, and showing that you have a handle on the trends is a great way to separate yourself from a crowded applicant pool. Another resource available at most universities is the PhD counsellor, who is there to help guide PhD students forward into their careers. Call the counselling office at your school and make an appointment.

A final word on formatting: **Make your name stand out!** Use all caps or bold or a larger font size. You should also put your name on a header or footer so it appears on every page of the CV. This is a must, as you want to avoid having your page 1 end up attached to another applicant's page 2.

If you're having trouble generating enough content for your CV, make a list of everything you've done that you're proud of. Classify the items on this into Academic, Professional, Community-Related, or Personal and find homes for them in the different sections of your CV.

Throughout your career, your CV should never be too far away from your desktop. It should be updated, added to, and reviewed regularly as you build your reputation in the academic and/or research world with each new position, publication, presentation, and study. Good luck!

Finally, I'd like to thank you for purchasing this book! If you enjoyed it or found it helpful, I'd greatly appreciate it if you'd take a moment to leave a review on Amazon. Thank you!

Made in the USA
Lexington, KY
18 June 2018